ANO • VOCAL • GUITAR

# DUMBO

All songs in this publication are the property of:

Bourne Co.
Music Publishers
**www.bournemusic.com**

Baby Mine
Casey Junior
Look Out for Mr. Stork
Pink Elephants on Parade
Song of the Roustabouts
When I See an Elephant Fly

ISBN 978-1-5400-5301-5

**BOURNE CO.**
New York

DISTRIBUTED BY

**HAL•LEONARD®**

Visit Hal Leonard Online at
**www.halleonard.com**

Contact us:
**Hal Leonard**
7777 West Bluemound Road
Milwaukee, WI 53213
Email: info@halleonard.com

In Europe, contact:
**Hal Leonard Europe Limited**
42 Wigmore Street
Marylebone, London, W1U 2RN
Email: info@halleonardeurope.com

In Australia, contact:
**Hal Leonard Australia Pty. Ltd.**
4 Lentara Court
Cheltenham, Victoria, 3192 Australia
Email: info@halleonard.com.au

# BABY MINE

Words by NED WASHINGTON
Music by FRANK CHURCHILL

# CASEY JUNIOR

Words by NED WASHINGTON
Music by FRANK CHURCHILL

# PINK ELEPHANTS ON PARADE

Words by NED WASHINGTON
Music by OLIVER WALLACE

**Vivace, in 2**

Look out! Look out! Pink el-e-phants on pa-rade. Here they come!
Look out! Look out! They're walk-ing a-round the bed, on their head,

Hip-pe-ty hop-pe-ty, they're here, and there, pink el-e-phants ev-'ry-where.
clip-pe-ty clop-pe-ty, ar-rayed in braid, pink el-e-phants on pa-

rade! What'll I do? What'll I do? What an un-u-su-al view!

# SONG OF THE ROUSTABOUTS

Words by NED WASHINGTON
Music by FRANK CHURCHILL

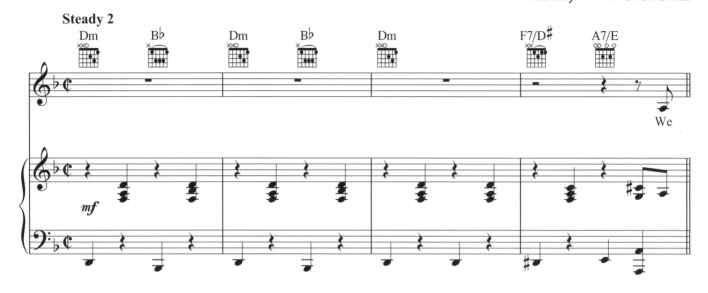

We

work all day and work all night. We nev-er learned to read or write. We're
oth-er folks have gone to bed, we slave un-til we're al-most dead. We're

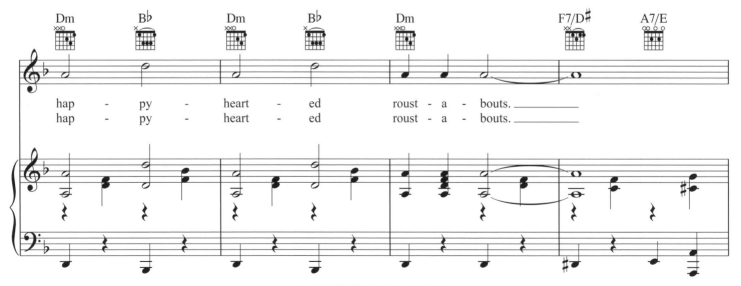

hap - py - heart - ed roust - a - bouts. _____
hap - py - heart - ed roust - a - bouts. _____

# WHEN I SEE AN ELEPHANT FLY

Words by NED WASHINGTON
Music by OLIVER WALLACE

**Moderate Swing**

Ho! Ho! When I think a-bout it,

Ho! Ho! I have to laugh. Ho! Ho!

Just to think a-bout it bends me right in half. I saw a
(I saw a)

19

# LOOK OUT FOR MR. STORK

Words by NED WASHINGTON
Music by FRANK CHURCHILL